Wisdom for Life, it's Child's Play

Inspiring you and your children to achieve more in life

Michael Moore

To Fiona

Best wishes

[handwritten signature] x

Wisdom for Life, it's Child's Play

Inspiring you and your children to achieve more in life

Written by Michael Moore

Polarity Publishing

Dedicated to Seeking Truth and Raising Consciousness

Orders: Please contact Polarity Publishing via the email address:
Orders@polaritypublishing.co.uk

ISBN: 978-1-9995810-1-5

First published 2019

Contents

Inspiration...
An introduction to 'Wisdom for Life, It's Child's Play'

Inspiring you and your children to achieve more in life

My objective in writing this book is to help everyone of us, but primarily children, to live a more fulfilling, happy and successful life and to achieve more of what we really want.

It is our birth right to be happy and to share in the surrounding abundance; generally as small children, we know nothing else.

Unfortunately, as we start to grow up, our parents, teachers and those around us, inadvertently kill the spirit within us bit by bit. They may mean well and want us to be safe and to learn the 'rules of life', but our spirit is suppressed and the light of our creative instinct is snuffed out.

It can take a lifetime to rekindle the light and in many cases some of us don't find it at all.

How sad to live a life that is unfulfilled, always hoping that things will change for the better.

Happily, there are ways we can change things; effective ways that are, in essence, very simple but do require an element of commitment and perseverance.

Having studied human psychology and personal development for over forty-five years I have been fascinated by what makes us tick as human beings and how some people live successful lives and others struggle.

There is no doubt we have all struggled at times, but that is just how life goes. It is what we do to cope with this and how we can improve our lives that I find so interesting.

Whether we want financial success, better health, better relationships, better this or better that, or just want to feel good about ourselves and those around us, all this can be achieved.

And it is not a massive shift, it is done by increasing our effort from 49% to 51%, that critical point from negative to positive; a subtle shift. It is doing a lot of little things that when added up make a huge difference overall.

There is a lot of advice out there which can be very confusing. Who do we listen to and how do we do it?

All I would say to this is, listen and watch and see what resonates with you, what your intuition tells you. As human beings we have far more ability than we think we have. We are born with all the answers within us; we just need to access them. I will share my thoughts and ideas that I have found helpful as we go through the book.

Just for now though, I urge you to have an open mind and believe that everything in life can be achieved; to have a mind that is open to everything and closed to nothing.

> *Life's battles don't always go to the stronger or faster man. But*
> *sooner or later the man who wins is the man who thinks he can.*
> Vince Lombardi

What is Holding us Back?

The route to all success need not be difficult. There are ways to achieve all that we want in life, we just need to take a different route, a simpler route to the one we are taught to take.

Chapter One

What Is Holding Us Back?

So where do we start?
What is holding us back from achieving what we want in life? What is stopping us from getting to the next level?

How can we have a more fulfilling life? What do we need to do?

We could list dozens of things, but here are some common excuses that prevent us from moving forward:

'I have no confidence'. 'I'm not clever enough'.
'I don't have the necessary educational qualifications'. 'I'm too young' or, 'I'm too old'.
'I've experienced bullying'. 'People say I can't do it'.
'My parents, teachers and those around me are negative about what can be achieved'.
'People don't understand me'. 'People reject me'.
'I don't know what I want'.
'I lack motivation and enthusiasm'. 'I don't have any money'
'I'm in the wrong job'.
'People won't like me if l am successful'.
'I tried it once and failed'.

Perhaps you may think of some more statements to add to the list; this is a good exercise and will highlight your blocks. It is also a great place to start.

As a child I suffered from most of the above; I was painfully shy and had a stammer, therefore communication was a big problem. I went to boarding school at the age of 8, far away from my parents and hugs and kisses. Although this was far from ideal for me as a shy child, I gradually learnt to fend for myself and become independent.

However, I left boarding school at the age of 12 when my father was taken ill suddenly and sadly died two weeks later.

None of this was good for my self-confidence, but I had to overcome it. Fortunately, my mother was a great inspiration to me. As a single parent, her determination amidst adversity to keep our family together and provide for us all, was a great lesson in perseverance and one from which we all benefited.

When I was 13 years old, I had to earn my own pocket money, so I went out cleaning cars on Saturday mornings. I guess this was my first stab at being self-employed.

Through this I learnt to be responsible, respectful and punctual. I also learnt the value of money, not only from my point of view, but also that of my car owning customers; they expected a good job done.

At age 17 I realised that if I wanted to progress in life it was up to me, so I worked diligently towards self-improvement and potential success.

I started my own Financial Services business at age 25, my job was all about communicating with people on a daily basis.

I also began studying human psychology. I studied dozens of books on personal development and overcoming adversity and was fascinated when reading other peoples' success stories. I listened to tapes and CDs, watched DVDs and attended courses on self-improvement and public speaking.

I was now age 35 and ten years into building my business, and also gathering my armory on what was needed to be successful, and how to achieve more of what I wanted.

I worked long hours and as a result became very stressed. This was exacerbated by moving house and taking on a huge financial commitment.

What I didn't realise was that we need a balance in life and success is not just financial, it's family, it's having loving relationships and very importantly, it's having good health.

Also, it's not just about us, it's how we interact and help others, it's having a goal in life that's bigger than us.

I was then given a life changing moment.

One of my mother's friends gave me a book called 'God is my Witness' by Ted Fricker.

Ted Fricker was a healer, just an ordinary man who realised that he had the gift of healing, particularly treating back complaints. His story is amazing; he has healed everyone from everyday people to celebrities and royalty.

I read his book almost in one go and realised that I too wanted to help people and be a healer myself. Maybe not of the physical body like Ted Fricker, but a healer of minds.

I suppose that's why I'm particularly interested in our conscious and subconscious minds. More on this in a later chapter.

I was fortunate enough to meet Ted Fricker some years later and although the meeting was brief, it was truly inspiring.

One thing I have always been passionate about is overcoming my own adversities so that I have a story to tell, that in itself can be inspiring to others.

I have learnt a lot over the years and have always been passionate about helping others, so in 2010 I was inspired to write my first book:

'What To Do When All Else Fails and How To Turn Your Life Around' (1)

I've tried to teach these principles to my own children and now my grandchildren, as this was passed down from my parents.

I learnt through people I admired that we can be successful in all aspects of life and still be a nice person, to be kind and thoughtful to others and in the process feel good about ourselves.

I've learnt also that any struggles we go through in life and that we overcome, gives us the desire to help others, that feeling of empathy with other people and their struggles.

I believe that what I've learned over 45 years can be refined into simple, workable techniques that we can use to become successful and improve all aspects of our lives.

As a result of my experience you can bypass all those years of study and start to implement the ideas immediately and achieve some truly amazing results, with the least amount of effort. Your commitment is to take action on a continuous basis with determination and of course, enjoy the journey.

If I can do it, anyone can do it:

It really is 'Child's Play'.

.

Setting **Goals**

Having a definite goal or purpose in life, can make all the difference between a successful life or just existing. The difference in the effort required can be very little.

Chapter Two

Setting Goals

If we know what we want in life and have a passion to achieve it, whatever it is, it can be fulfilled. So, setting a goal is a very good place to start.

It helps us to define exactly what we want so that all our thought and energy can be focused in one direction.

If we don't know what we want yet, that's okay. There are techniques to bring this to the surface which we will discuss later. For now though, let's focus on our specific goals.

Our goals should be put in writing, written in the present tense, and with as much clear detail as possible. By writing down our goals with clarity, we become more focused and motivated whenever we read our statement. We also engage the creative parts of our brain which then starts to help us achieve our goals.

The use of the present tense brings our goal into the NOW, so that our subconscious mind can go to work on it immediately. We will look at how our subconscious mind works in the next chapter.

The more detail we write down the more real our goals become and the quicker they can be manifested into reality.

Our statement should be read (and later memorised) every day, ideally, first thing in the morning and particularly last thing at night when our mind is quiet and receptive to ideas planted therein. Also, it should be repeated several times during the day.

The more we can 'live' our dreams the better.

Harvard Business School conducted a study of 100 students on the subject of goal setting, to assess how written and planned for goals affect later outcomes in life.

Prior to graduation it was determined that 84% of the entire class had set no goals at all, 13% of the class had set goals but no concrete plans and 3% of the class had both written goals and concrete plans.

10 years later the 13% of the class that had set written goals but had no concrete plans were making twice as much money as the 84% of the class who had no goals at all.

However, the 3% of the class that had both written goals and concrete plans, were making 10 times as much as the rest of the 97% of the class.

There is power in being organised.

As we read our written statement, we should visualise our goal as clearly as possible and feel the feeling as if we are already in possession of the end result. Interestingly enough, our subconscious mind cannot tell the difference between something real and something imagined, so we can take advantage of this fact.

Visualising and creating the feeling of actually being in possession of our goals will stimulate our subconscious mind to accelerate finding ways of transforming our thoughts into reality.

Many studies have been carried out on how the subconscious works.

Under hypnosis an individual was told that his finger would be touched with a red-hot poker. In reality his finger was touched with a pencil but because he believed what he was told, the finger blistered. Another example was that of an athlete who was hooked up to sophisticated bio feedback equipment and instructed to run a race in his mind. As he did this, his muscles fired up in exactly the same sequence as if the race was being run physically.

Our imagination is such a powerful tool that it can bring into reality all that we want by way of its proper use.

Einstein said: "Imagination is more powerful than knowledge".

A further thought here is the use of GRATITUDE which I refer to often.

Although we may be asking for more things in our lives, being grateful for what we have, however small, puts us in the right frame of mind and the right vibration to receive what we ask for.

We can only receive what we want by having a positive frame of mind and building belief that it will appear.

So how can we find out what we want in life if we are not sure at this stage what our goals are?

We may have general goals or indeed no definite goals at all, so this could be true of many of us. It may be that we just want to feel happier than we are now, to be content and basically have peace of mind, which in itself is a very worthwhile goal and from this we can develop a truly meaningful life.

Having said earlier that as human beings we have all the answers within us, we need a simple technique to bring these thoughts to the surface.

The way we can do this is to calm our mind and ask simple questions, for example:

"What would make me really happy?"
"How can I be successful in something that is meaningful?"
"How can I bring to the surface my true God-given talents?"
"What do I need to do to be successful in life?"
"How can I be of service to others?" "What is my purpose in life?"

Ask, and expect to receive the answers, and repeat as often a necessary.

This may be an oversimplification, but a few moments regularly spent in quiet time, focusing on these simple questions will have a dramatic and profound effect on us and our future well-being. It can help achieve overall success in every aspect of our lives.

We may not find that answers to our requests come instantly but carried out consistently and with determination to obtain the answers, the truth will show itself to us. I've used this technique to get answers to everyday situations and it works like magic.

Practicing this routine daily, particularly last thing at night, can bring about very interesting results. What we are doing here is using the power of our minds which we will see can create all that we desire, it is not common knowledge, but by using some simple techniques we can unlock the true potential of our minds with ease and flow.

OUR Conscious *and* *Subconscious* Mind

> *Our mind is the most powerful force in the Universe and can achieve for us all we desire. If we learn to use it well it will amaze **us***

Chapter Three

Our Conscious and Subconscious Mind

How our mind works is a fascinating subject, and many wiser people than I, have studied it in great detail. Everything I have read on the subject illustrates to me that it is the greatest force in the Universe.

'You become what you think about most of the time'.
Earl Nightingale (known as the father of modern-day inspiration).

'Whatever the mind of man can conceive and believe, it can achieve'.
Napoleon Hill (author of 'Think and Grow Rich').

'Thoughts are things'.
Albert Einstein

'We are what we think, all that we are arises with our thoughts, with our thoughts, we make the world'.
Buddha

'For as he thinketh in his heart, so is he'.
Proverbs 23:7

Our thoughts are dynamic and have great power and if used correctly can create real magic.

We have a conscious mind and a subconscious mind. The conscious mind is the thinking mind – we could liken it to the computer operator. We can choose what we think about, therefore we have total free will to think what we like. This puts us apart from all other living creatures.

The thoughts we have are then passed over to our subconscious mind, which is the creative mind. Anything planted in our mind will become rooted there, whether it is a positive or negative thought.

Liken this to a seed planted in the soil; the seed will grow into the plant from which it originally came from. The soil does not question what seed is planted; it just produces whatever is planted in it.

Our subconscious mind is the same, it reproduces the thought planted in it, good thoughts or bad thoughts, positive thoughts or negative thoughts.

It is no wonder that if we think bad thoughts or negative thoughts, the results of those thoughts affect our lives. Bearingin mind we have total control over what we think, it is our responsibility to live to our full potential.

The process is simple, the trick is to train our conscious mind to think of health, wealth, happiness, joy and abundance. What we thought about previously has manifested in our lives today, therefore, to change our future we need to retrain ourminds from today.

By holding in our mind what we want in life, as precisely as possible and visualising this with the feeling that it already exists, we will automatically manifest what we desire for the future.

We must then guard against any negative thoughts in the meantime that could uproot our seed of thought and damage its growth.

We need to be aware that every thought that starts in our conscious mind eventually manifests in our subconscious mind and then becomes reality.

This process is a Universal Law of nature. We don't necessarily need to know how it works; we just need to believe it does. Like the seed planted in the ground the seed itself does the work, it knows what it will grow into with the help of the soil that nurtures it.

The unforeseen force of nature IS the force that turns the world and holds the Universe together; it beats our heart and grows the grass, we do not question it, we just expect it to work.

All we have to do is to hold the vision of what we want, the feeling of it already being in existence and then expect it to be drawn to us. Let us take our mind off what we don't want and on to what we do want.

Our subconscious mind is totally impersonal, it does not think, it just carries out the instruction given to it by our conscious mind. Like the soil into which a seed is planted, it produces the plant from the seed without question.

Our job now is to let go of the thought and allow our subconscious mind to produce the result unhindered. Our mind will find the solution to our request in the most efficient and effective way without any further input or hindrance from us.

Let our mind therefore do the work; our job is just to think correctly and sow the seeds. This after all is a partnership between us and the Universe.

The *Law* of *Attraction*

(How we attract everything into our lives).

We can attract everything we want in life by using the simple Laws of the Universe. These are available to us all. Take full advantage of these and watch the magic unfold!

Chapter Four

The Law of Attraction

The Law of Attraction and its values have been with us since time began.

Hundreds of years ago, it is believed that Buddha wanted it to be known that – 'What you become is what you have thought'.

A great many men and women in the history books left their mark on the world by using the Law of Attraction.

Many well-loved poets, artists, scientists and thinkers such as Shakespeare, Blake, Einstein and others I have mentioned in this book all convey this message through their many works.

Today, many people we follow who are in the public eye also use the Law of Attraction.

We have heard the saying 'like attracts like', well this is all down to vibration and frequency or energy.

Let me explain:

We live in a vibrational world. Everything vibrates at some level, on a higher or lower frequency. Our bodies vibrate, buildings vibrate, the earth vibrates and rocks vibrate.

The lighter an object is the higher the frequency of vibration, the denser an object is the lower the frequency of vibration. If we now look at our thoughts, they too vibrate and are on different frequencies depending on whether we have positive thoughts or negative thoughts. Interesting!

Thoughts are therefore dynamic and are in a state of change all the time as we have seen in the Albert Einstein quote: 'Thoughts are Things'.

If we think positively, we emit a higher vibration, if we think negatively, we emit a lower vibration.

On the basis that 'like attracts like' if we want to attract good things into our lives, we need to lift our vibration. In other words, if we lift our thoughts to a more positive level, to feel that 'good feeling', this in turn will attract what we want in life rather than what we don't want.

In practice the principle is simple but does require strength of mind. But before long, with commitment, positive thinking will become a habit, and we will achieve positive results.

Having a worthwhile goal or goals in life and the passion to achieve them, can give us the momentum to keep our thoughts more positive than negative.

Most importantly, we are responsible for whatever we attract into our lives and do have more control than we think we have.

We cannot necessarily stop negative thoughts or negative things happening to us, but we can take control of how we deal with them and by how we think and respond.

Any negativity can be reversed by proper use of our mind. Similarly, anything we want in life can be achieved in the same way. Have faith in this, it really works.

> *'Change your thoughts and change your life'.*
> Dr. Wayne Dyer (renowned author and inspirational speaker).

Our *Paradigm,*
Our *Conditioning*

Our conditioning can be changed almost overnight, from wondering if we can achieve, to expecting everything in life to be attainable and all by using simple techniques.

Chapter Five

Our Paradigm, Our Conditioning.

One of the main reasons we think as we do is because of our paradigms or our conditioning.

Our conditioning starts from when we are born and is governed by our parents, our teachers, our friends, our relatives and the people we associate with, as well as from television, newspapers and social media. In fact, everybody and everything we come into contact with throughout our lives, influences us and builds our paradigms.

Unfortunately, the majority of our conditioning is negative, so it can take a real effort to change how we think and ultimately how we live.

We certainly CAN change our outlook, it just means we need to be that much more determined to live the way we want to live, rather than how others think we should live.

We can change our paradigms by the proper use of our mind and although we don't really know how our mind works, we can take it on good faith that it can be done.

How electricity works is somewhat of a mystery, as is the way mobile phones work. How is it that words and pictures can appear on our mobile phones in a matter of seconds sent from halfway round the world? Amazing! Yet we accept that these modern-day inventions, mostly without a second thought.

I'm sure if we went back in time, say a hundred years, and tried to explain to someone the workings of a mobile phone it would be impossible for them to grasp the concept.

Similarly, if we think forward a hundred years from now we cannot really know what exciting technological developments lie ahead. It is reasonable therefore to assume that our minds have powers far beyond our understanding, even now.

We use technology without really understanding how it works so why not use our mind more fully and take advantage of its enormous power.

In my book 'What To Do When All Else Fails' I gave the example of a Vietnamese prisoner of war who was in captivity for a period of several years. He had been an average golfer in the past and to keep himself sane he visualised playing his round of golf over and over again in his mind, playing every shot to perfection.

On his return to civilisation and after a period of recuperation he returned to the golf course. He played his first round of golf to par, knocking more than 20 strokes off his last game several years previously. This illustrates the power of the mind and how it can be used to our advantage.

We are totally governed by what we think we can achieve and by our erroneous belief system. This is brought about by our conditioning, and our paradigms.

For a moment, let us consider what we could achieve.

To put this into perspective, let us say for example that our vision of what we think we can achieve, let us call it our 'radar', is 1 square meter. By pushing the barriers out this can be expanded to perhaps 2 square meters or even 100 square meters. By imagining this, we realise the previous limits we put on our achievements was what we THOUGHT we could achieve.

If our mind has infinite power, which I believe it has, moving forward inch by inch could be accelerated dramatically.

Steven Scott in his publication 'Mentored by a Millionaire' (2), puts forward the theory that we can take quantum leaps by looking at what we might initially think was impossible to achieve and turn this over to our mind with the belief that it COULD be achieved. After all, our subconscious mind does not think in terms of size, anything goes, big or small. It is up to us to ask. It is our conscious mind that intervenes and says: "It can't be done".

By keeping an open mind on any situation and not blocking the outcome with our negative thinking, our mind can solve large problems as well as small ones. There is no limit to what we can achieve.

Our subconscious mind therefore can tackle any problem and produce the answer in the most efficient and effective way. This is how the Wright brothers conquered flying, and how Thomas Edison produced the electric light bulb and countless other inventions that we take for granted today.

All new inventions were seemingly impossible before they were invented.

So, what is stopping us now? Rather than focusing on what we think we can't achieve, let us turn it around and do the impossible. 'The Secret' is a best-selling self-help book by Rhonda Byrne (3) It is based on the earlier film of the same name which is available as a DVD. In the film, Jack Canfield author of 'Chicken Soup for the Soul' (4) recounts how he used this principle of letting go of his limitations to increase his income from $8,000 to $100,000 in a year.

Jack at this time was mentored by W. Clement Stone, one of the wealthiest men in America and a great inspiration to many. Stone told Jack he must have a goal that was something much larger than he thought he could achieve, and then he would soon know that the Law of Attraction worked. He asked Jack what he would like to earn. Jack replied that he would like to earn $100,000 within 12 months. Jack felt this was a tall order as he was only earning $8000 a year up until this time. Nevertheless, he took Stone's advice. He wrote three more O's on a $100 bill and placed it on the ceiling over his bed so that he could see it every morning upon waking. He started off by visualising his goal and how he would feel once his dream became a reality.

Nothing happened for a few weeks and then in the shower Jack had an inspired thought. He had written a book, and he thought that if he could sell 400,000 copies of his book for 25 cents each this would give him $100,000. But how was he going to do this? He had noticed a copy of the National Enquirer magazine in his local supermarket and somehow this sparked something in him. He thought that his book would appeal to its readers, and they would undoubtedly want to buy it.

Six weeks later he was giving a talk to 600 teachers which seemed to go well. Afterwards, a journalist came up to him.

"That was a great talk, I'd like to write an article on you" she said, and Jack asked who she wrote for.

"I'm freelance, but I sell most of my work to the National Enquirer" was the reply!

The upshot of the story was that Jack sold almost 400,000 copies of his book and made a little over $92,000 in the allotted time.

His wife then asked whether the same thinking would work to achieve the sum he had dreamed of – $1,000,000.

Jack's reply was: "Why not?"

Sometime later, he received a cheque for $1,000,000 from his publishers for his first 'Chicken Soup for the Soul' book.

There are countless amazing stories similar to this that are available to inspire all of us to greater achievements. It's worth immersing ourselves in these stories along our journey to our own success.

The *Next Phase* in *Setting Goals*

We do not need to know all the steps to achieve what we want in life, just take the first one with faith and all will be revealed to us along the way.

Chapter Six

The Next Phase in Setting Goals

Once we have a written statement of what we want to achieve, we must then implement the second stage and that is to have a plan of how we will achieve this.

Our goal maybe to get a job, play an instrument, write a book or, like Jack Canfield, promote a book we have already written. Perhaps we want to get into a better relationship.

Maybe we would like to start a business, take a trip of a lifetime, win an Olympic medal, or any medal for that matter; perhaps we dream of pulling off that big deal, passing an exam or getting a degree.

We need something tangible to work towards, a track to run on, a starting point for our journey; somewhere to take the first step. Our plan is about how we are going to start achieving our goal, the initial steps we need to take.

The third stage is literally to take action. Nothing will happen unless we are in motion, ready or not, we can perfect our plan along the way.

As the saying goes, 'You may be on the right road but if you don't move you will get run over'.

By taking action we are then moving forward and can easily change direction if necessary, our plan may change, but we must always keep our goal in mind.

We then start the fourth and very important process, following the route between where we are now and where we want to go. Once in motion however, the Universe takes over, and the route will be shown to us.

I must admit I struggled for many years with stage four. I used to think that I had to map out all the steps to my goal one by one; this delayed my action, and meant I took longer to achieve my goals.

It is impossible to see the whole journey at the start. Just like when we use satellite navigation, we have a goal in mind that is our destination, and we have a plan to drive from one point to another. We then take action by starting the car and putting it into gear. We are then set to go.

The journey or stage four will be shown to us, bit by bit along the way. And this is the MAGIC of life.

Once we have mastered stages 1, 2 and 3 which is our input into the journey of life, the Universe will prompt us as we go along by intuition and inspiration.

As long as we do our bit and hold the vision of our goal with passion and determination, everything we want in life can be achieved.

Yes, there will be obstacles along the way, but this is where we must remain steadfast to our cause.

If we remember that goal setting is an ongoing activity and not just a means to an end, we can keep ourselves on track. It is a good idea to make time to review our goals regularly.

When we keep our end destination in sight, even if our action plan changes a little along the way, the motivation will stay with us.

If we have a really worthwhile goal or goals, all can be achieved.

Believe
and
Succeed

Belief is the missing link between where we are now and where we want to go. Attach ourselves to nature and see the miracle work.

Chapter Seven

Believe and Succeed

The next stage in the process is to believe that we can achieve more in life and this is where most of us need help.

If we have not already achieved something we want, how are we going to believe we can?

There has to be certain amounts of blind faith, in other words, do it anyway.

Let's just take a simple example.

If we plant a seed in the ground, water and nurture its growth and keep the ground weed free, in time we will see a plant appear. If we plant a sunflower seed we know we will get a sunflower. We have faith and know the flower will grow.

The same is true when we plant the seed of thought in our mind. If we look after that thought in a positive way and don't allow ourselves to have doubts about what we wish for materialising, then it will appear exactly as we want it to.

After we plant the seed in the ground, we do not dig up the seed regularly to see how it is doing. We trust that in the appropriate time it will appear as a green shoot then fully grow into a sunflower.

It is the natural way of cause and effect.

Similarly, we accept without question the force of gravity; so too we can accept and believe certain things that cannot be explained or seen.

Belief is a prerequisite to achievement, so if we don't believe we can achieve something in the future, we probably won't even bother to try.

It is with belief and faith that we start out on a Journey to achievement, with all the hope that we can muster.

Nobody has ever achieved anything in life without the belief that it could work out OK.

All the great inventors had the belief that their experiments would bear fruit.

We must have faith in our ability. We may start feeling a little shaky but by beginning the process we gain confidence and momentum.

We can learn the lessons from people who have overcome adversity and who have achieved more than they first thought they could.

At the age of 26, Bob Proctor, of 'The Secret' fame, didn't believe in anything. Then a man called Ray Stanford gave him a book by Napoleon Hill called 'Think and Grow Rich' (5). Although Bob was skeptical, he had faith in Ray Stanford and so he took the book and read it.

This very act totally changed Bob's life. With faith and new belief, his income went from $6,000 a year to $175,000 and then to $1M in three years. He is now one of the great philosophers of our age.

If we look back at some things that we thought were difficult or even impossible to achieve, but we DID achieve them, then this will give us the confidence and belief that we can achieve more in the future.

> *'If you can believe, all things are possible to he who believes'.*
> Mark Chapter 9:23

> *'Believe and your belief will create the fact'.*
> William James

Put it to the test and go for it anyway, you will be amazed what can be achieved with belief.

Building Belief

Belief can be mastered by one simple word, GRATITUDE. It is the foundation of life and all achievement.

Chapter Eight

Building Belief

There are some simple techniques to build belief and probably the most effective one is acknowledging the feeling of GRATITUDE: being grateful for what we already have.

In his book 'The Science of Getting Rich', author Wallace Wattles (6) says: "Faith is born of gratitude, the grateful mind continuously expects good things and expectation becomes faith".

So being grateful for what we have will attract more of what we want. As we have seen, what we focus on is what we get.

A simple technique to reinforce this is to write down ten things we are grateful for every day. These can be big things or little things; even mentioning that we hear the birds singing or noting that someone said something kind to us.

It really doesn't matter what it is as long as it fills our mind with grateful thanks. If we do this every day, within 21 days our lives will take on a dramatic shift, encouraging us to commit to do this every day of our lives.

It is really just a question of realising what makes us feel good and feel better about what's going on in our lives.

We can also start to seek out and be with positive people. Being in their company can have a dramatic effect on our well-being as we take on their higher vibration. There is too much negativity in the world, so we have to guard against this at all costs.

If we get excited about what we want to achieve, and have a passion that is unshakable, this will work wonders for our belief system.

With our new techniques, we can learn to focus on what we want, not what we don't want. There is a tendency in life to think about all the things that can go wrong and this will derail any ambition we have.

Form a good habit of always expecting the best. If a negative thought comes into our mind, consciously change it for a positive thought. It does take practice but very soon this will become our natural way of thinking.

The only way to push out a negative thought is with a positive thought.

Also, we should always follow our intuition. By holding in our mind what we want in life, intuitions come to us, generally when we least expect them. This is what happened to Jack Canfield.

We do have all the answers within us. We are built with all the necessary self-survival mechanisms; we just have tolearn how to access them.

There is a story of the Wise Old Man, who lived in a log cabin and used to sit on his veranda in a rocking chair. All the villagers used to come and ask him for his wisdom in solving their problems. After discussing their problems they always went away feeling they could take control of their worries.

We can use this as an analogy: The Wise Old Man is in fact our inner selves and we can visit him in our minds with any questions we are wrestling with. After a while we will find the answers we need.

So, in life, if we expect to find an answer, generally it will come to us. It is an interesting thought and one I've used for many years now and it certainly works.

The trick is to be relaxed enough to have the intuition for this method to work effectively. We will talk more on how to access this in the next chapter.

Affirmations are another excellent way to build belief and train our mind in a very positive way.

If we repeat certain phrases over and over, this will be burnt into our mind and in time a state of real positivity can be reached.

It is rather like the athlete who trains daily to reach his full potential and then once he has reached it continues training to maintain peak performance.

Our mind is the same, repetition builds belief but unfortunately most of us don't train our mind effectively.

The question is, do we want success in our lives or not? Are we willing to pay the price?

Are we willing to train our minds consistently to achieve any and everything we want?

All the techniques are simple; they just need our commitment and perseverance to succeed.

We are all responsible for our own lives, not anyone else's, but our own first.

Once we become strong, particularly in our minds, we can then help others to become strong.

We are all put on this earth for a reason and that is to do the best we can, to be better people. In doing this we can then inspire others to help themselves.

It is our responsibility to do this and it is my mission to help others to achieve their full potential and then 'pay it forward'.

This really means that instead of paying someone back for a good deed, we do a good deed for someone else.

'Paying it forward' takes on all sorts of actions – it means aiding others who could use some help or who are in need of our care and assistance.

Any single one of us can effect changes that can affect many others as well as ourselves. This will require our determination and confidence.

It is interesting too, that by changing our thinking and our beliefs and eventually using our new mindset to help others, we become happier people.

Finally, to build belief, act as if it were impossible to fail. This is a very creative process.

If we really think about this, it is a self-fulfilling prophecy. By our actions we build a feeling within, and a feeling within, blended with a positive thought process, as we have seen, causes our mind to manifest what we think about.

Let us be the main character in our movie of life.

Feeling Good

Feeling good and being happy is our birthright, it doesn't have to be earned as it is already within us. Don't let life itself deprive us of it, which it can so easily do. The Choice is ours.

Chapter Nine

Feeling Good

So how do we feel good?

There are so many things in life that can affect how we feel. Feeling good is probably the most important state to cultivate and if we can master this, we will attract so many good things into our lives.

There are a number of obvious things we can do, for example eating well, taking exercise, being out in nature, indulging in hobbies such as music, dancing, painting, and creative activities. If we have pets, we know our dog is always pleased to see us even if other family members aren't!

Reading, listening to inspiring people, physical contact with others, hugs and kisses.

I heard a heart-warming story about a pair of prematurely born babies, one was strong but the other was unfortunately very weak and not expected to live. As a final act the nurses put the weaker child in the incubator and physically in contact with the stronger child. Through this very act the weaker child gained strength and survived.

We don't always realise how, as human beings, physical contact is so important for our well-being.

Laughter is also an amazing tonic. It is impossible to feel bad when we laugh.

Smiles and acts of kindness also go a long way to feeling good, for those who give, for those who receive and also any onlookers. We all benefit!

Sometimes we have to summon our inner strength during very bad times. When severe challenges occur we need to find inner belief to help us through.

During the terrible events of 9/11 and the collapse of the Twin Towers, there were glimmers of this. How did we all feel as onlookers when we saw the firefighters bring out survivors?

Amidst the tragedy, the firefighters were at least rewarded with the knowledge that they had saved peoples' lives, and the survivors were overwhelminglygrateful for being saved from the burning towers. And the whole world that watched felt compassion for the firefighters' heroic acts.

It is also important to do what WE want in life rather than what is expected of us by others.

We know what is best for us by using our internal guidance system which is personal only to us.

Our parents and teachers say they know what is best for us, and sometimes they do; when we are young we need certain boundaries for safety and well-being, but as we grow we need encouragement and the freedom of being allowed to think for ourselves.

So often we get distracted by what is going on around us and lose sight of what is really important. Every now and again it is good to take a step back and remember what is important.

We need to look inwardly to get the answers we need to all our questions, particularly in our own lives.

Let us go to the 'Wise old Man' inside us all for the answers.

Imagination *and* *dream* building

Let us build our dreams with our imagination, it is fun. It is what we did as a child. Let us go back to those simpler times and go forward with that childlike mentality.

Chapter Ten

Imagination and Dream Building

Einstein said: "Imagination is everything. It is the preview of life's coming attractions."

As children we have a great imagination, we can picture anything we wish, there are no barriers for a child, anything goes.

Slowly but surely, with the best of intentions, our parents and teachers start to unwittingly dismantle this wonderful world of 'anything is possible'.

We then spend a lifetime in trying to regain the wonderment we had as a child.

For many of us our true potential is never reached.

Wayne Dyer, one of the most inspirational people of our time said: "Don't die with your music still in you".

My mission is to help reignite the flame within us, before it is finally snuffed out. For our children, we need to light the flame and be sure it glows brightly from an early age and doesn't dim.

Let us go back to visualisation and use our imagination in the way that we were meant to use it. By visualising what we want in life and feeling passionate about it, we know how we will feel when we receive it and we can then attract all that we desire.

The technique of using vision boards is a very effective way of keeping our vision in full view so that our mind can work on our goals, desires and wishes constantly.

We can make up a vision board very simply. If we select pictures of all the things we want, perhaps a house, a car or a dream holiday, and glue them onto a board, perhaps adding some special words, like love, health etc., we can leave it in a prominent place and look at it often. This helps to reinforce our belief that these things will come to us.

Going back to 'The Secret', John Assaraf gives the example of his own vision board which depicted, amongst other things, the type of house he would like to own.

Having moved several times in five years his vision board had been packed away in a box for all of this time.

He finally bought the house of his dreams and one day his son came into his study where the packing case was stored.

"What's in the packing case?" His son asked him. John replied – "My vision board".

"What's a vision board?"

John replied – "Pictures of things I'd like to own".

With that he opened the box and got out the vision board. To his absolute surprise the picture of the house on the vision board was the exact same house he had bought, not a similar one but the actual house, and he didn't even realise it was the house he had bought.

That is the power of vision boards!

Also, positive words that can motivate and inspire us are also an important step in reaching our goals.

Anything that motivates and inspires us should go on our vision board and we should have it visible to us on a daily basis. The fact that it is in view, even if not studied regularly, means our mind will go to work in attracting what we want.

We can even write down the sort of person we want to be in life. By writing down our thoughts and aspirations, we are more than halfway to achieving them.

Also, writing down questions to which we want answers is a technique I've used for many years. I always make sure to add a 'thank you' at the end and the expectation that the right answer will appear. This may seem 'off the wall' but it works.

There was an interesting person in America called Edgar Cayce, a clairvoyant. With no medical experience he would diagnose peoples' ailments and put forward cures.

Cayce would write down peoples' symptoms and place them under his bed where he kept all his medical books, which incidentally he had never read.

In the morning he would be inspired to come up with a cure for his 'patients'. (This may not be suitable for everyone but it's an interesting story!).

We really don't know how the mind works or what unseen forces there are out there, but the more I read and study these matters and more particularly, use them myself, the more I see their validity.

There are easier ways to live and get results than perhaps are initially apparent to us, so why struggle when these ways are open to us all?

We are all conditioned by our upbringing and the environment in which we live, and all the influences we receive on a daily basis. This is our paradigm. What we must try and do is to change our paradigm.

Any habit can be changed in about 14 to 21 days. New habits can therefore be formed by changing the way we think.

It is true that if we want to change our outcome, we must firstly change our current methods. This may require ongoing input from us, but certainly it is well worth the effort if we want to achieve more in life.

Life is really an attitude of mind, how we see things from our perspective. None of us are right or wrong but if things are not working the way we want them to then we must change our attitude, change the way we think, change what we put out there in the world.

There was an interesting story about a man at the city gate.

He asked the gatekeeper: "What are the people like in your city?"

The gatekeeper replied: "Well, what are the people like where you come from?'

The man said: "Where I come from the people are not very nice, they're grumpy and not very friendly, I've got no time for them." The gatekeeper said: "Yes they're very similar here," and with that the man went away.

The next day another man arrived at the city gate and asked the gatekeeper: "What are the people like in your city?"

The gatekeeper replied: "Well, what are they like where you come from?"

The man said: "Where I come from the people are very pleasant and friendly and everyone helps each other, it's a nice place to live."

The gatekeeper said: " Well, they are much the same in here, come in."

You see, what we hold in our mind and how we act is reflected back to us in life. We attract things, as we have seen previously, that are on the same vibration.

Good thoughts and deeds attract a good response, bad thoughts and deeds attract a bad response. Negative feelings are a habit; depression is brought about by consistent negative thoughts and feelings.

'Change our thoughts and change our lives'.

Positive *Vocabulary*

how words influence our lives.

Words can build or destroy, use them wisely; this will be a good habit to develop.

Chapter Eleven

Positive Vocabulary

The words we use have a definite influence on our lives, probably more than we appreciate.

We use words to communicate with others and as we live in a vibrational world, words are just as vibrational and have a life of their own.

Using certain words sets up a vibration within us that can change our feelings and therefore our outcome. For example, if we want to experience JOY repeat the word JOY over and over again and the feeling of joy will be projected into our whole being.

Any positive state can be induced with the use of positive words. Also bear in mind that the same is true if we use negative words, which we tend to do without thinking: "I'm sick and tired with this" or "You're a pain in the neck." By using these words, we similarly induce and perpetuate negative feelings.

Dr Omoto, a Japanese author and entrepreneur realised that human consciousness has an effect on the molecular structure of water.

He performed experiments to show how adding words to water brought astounding results. Positive words such as LOVE, PEACE and GRATITUDE were written on labels on beakers of water and then the water was crystallized. The crystals were put under a microscope which showed that they were beautifully formed in amazing patterns.

Similarly, negative words were written on the labels, such as HATE, ANGER and FEAR and this time the crystals were shown to be completely deformed and disfigured.

If thoughts and words can do that to water, imagine what our thoughts and words can do to us, bearing in mind that our bodies are made up of more than 60% water.

We have around 60,000 thoughts a day, most of which, if we let our mind wander, are negative.

By controlling our minds and what we think and say, it can have a dramatic effect on our lives. Such a simple solution will bring about change, although we must use self-control to achieve this.

The cells of our body are regenerating constantly; some organs in a matter of days, with denser parts taking longer. Our body is totally regenerated every 7 years.

Why then with a new body do we still become unwell? I think it is all down to our thinking.

Knowing that the body regenerates, it is important to use this amazing opportunity Mother Nature has given us to ensure we give our bodies the best possible nourishment, both of the body and of the soul, so that it can regenerate in a healthy way.

Our mental well-being is dynamic. With positive thinking we can feel relatively confident in ourselves and have positive self esteem. In turn, some studies show that personality traits such as optimism or pessimism can affect many areas of our health and well-being.

Positive thinking is a key part of effective stress management and reduces the harmful effects of stress on the body.

There are so many reasons why our thinking and the words we use should be in check; it is our responsibility.

How *Long* will *It* Take?

Everything can be achieved far more quickly than we think it can. By changing our focus onto what we want and holding that vision steadfastly, we will be amazed at the results.

Chapter Twelve

How Long Will It Take?

The more focused we are the quicker our positive results will appear. We must do our bit, as described in the preceding chapters, and the Universe will do its bit.

It is a partnership, and we don't have to do it alone. Equally, we must have a definite input and take action. Everything happens at the right time in the right way.

Belief is paramount and 99% of all achievement comes from the thought process behind it. Even negative results are nature's way of teaching us. We generally grow through adversity and not giving in to failure. In the words of Winston Churchill: "Never, never, never give up".

If we do as much as we can each and every day, our lives will be successful.

It is said that, 'Success is a journey not a destination' which is one of my favourite quotes.

You see, if we achieve our goals the 'wrong way' by being stressed and unhappy, why do we think that we will change once our goal is achieved? No way! If on the other hand we are happy and have peace of mind along the way, actually reaching our ultimate goal becomes less important. Interesting!

In reality, we can't actually attract the good things in life if we don't raise our vibration by having a better feeling about life.

Our focus therefore should be on feeling good anyway, having gratitude for what we do have, and this will give us the momentum to attract more.

Do we think that by employing the techniques laid down in this book we could start to reverse most of what is holding us back? Let us look at our 'blockages' and see where we can make a difference:

'I am lacking in confidence'.

If we have lacked confidence in the past our confidence must surely grow with our new techniques, as we are now in control of our destiny. We don't need to be clever or academically qualified; we will have many other very practical attributes.

'I am too young / too old'.

We may worry about age but age is actually irrelevant in achieving our goals in life, there are countless examples of many young and indeed older people who have achieved great things in their lives.

'I have suffered from bullying / I can' t do it / my parents and teachers and those around me are negative about my achievements / people don't understand me / I have faced rejection'.

What people think of us is largely unimportant on our journey towards success; by being successful we can actually bring them along with us.

'I lack motivation and enthusiasm / don't know what I want / I'm in the wrong job'.

With our new-found enthusiasm and motivation, we will find what is really important to us in life and this will give us our direction and passion.

'I don't have enough money'.

Satisfaction and money will flow to us with the abundance offered to us by the Universe.

'I tried it once and failed'.

And yes, we will stumble and fail along the way, but if our focus is always on our goals, this blended with passion and determination, will pull us through.

How determined are we to succeed and reach our potential as human beings? The rewards are enormous and can be so fulfilling.

My belief is that we can achieve anything in life according to how we THINK and how we use the simple techniques mentioned and indeed with the enormous power of our MIND.

Does This Stuff
Really Work?

This 'stuff' certainly does work. It will help us achieve that elusive state of mind called HAPPINESS and really is the only way to a better and more fulfilling life.

Chapter Thirteen

Does This Stuff Really Work?

You bet!
From my own experience and indeed countless examples of other peoples' lives I have known and read about; the answer is a resounding YES!

Let me tell you about my own experiences. My first job at the age of 18 was with an insurance company, where I worked as an office clerk. Our sales team had monthly and annual sales targets which were displayed on the office noticeboard.

This was a great lesson in goal setting for me at that age, and a system I continued to use early in my career, particularly when I started my own business at age the age of 25. As we have seen, setting goals is paramount to achieving what we want in life, thus giving us a definite focus.

Working in financial services we had the opportunity to meet many successful people and great inspirational writers, including many from America.

With such an inspirational base to work from, I started learning more and more about human psychology and how to be successful. I found it all-consuming.

I always had an annual target to work towards, broken down into monthly targets. It became part of my DNA.

I would start the year with my written target for that year, overlaid with my overall goals in life. I collected pictures of things I wanted to acquire;

the type of house I wanted to live in, a car maybe, a holiday, and many other things.

I also wrote down things I was concerned about and needed to be addressed that year and added the list to my file. I still have that file and when I look back, most of what I wrote down has been achieved and the things I worried about didn't amount to anything. That was fascinating, as we all worry too much about stuff that generally doesn't happen.

I always had a plan to work on and when business got difficult, I had more plans. We certainly went through many ups and downs, but I just kept going, always believing that things would get better and generally they did.

I relied on all the inspirational offerings I could lay my hands on, particularly to expand my vision and achieve more, but also to give me confidence when things got tough. It was a great source of support and still is.

I always tried to keep up my positive thinking, although at times I got bogged down with life and lapsed a little. When these times occurred I would go back to basics, re-discipline myself and keep up my mental training. When I got back to it things always improved.

It is human nature to lapse from time to time, but it was a great lesson to me to keep up that mental training and get back to peak performance.

A very notable time in my business career was the period of the worldwide financial crisis of 2007/8. By 2009 all businesses were suffering including mine.

It was at that time a friend introduced me to 'The Secret'. This book and the accompanying DVD based on the Law of Attraction encapsulated all the philosophies I had learnt over the years and more. It proved to be a real tonic at a time when I needed a new injection of inspiration.

Not only did I pull myself out of those negative financial times we were all going through, but I decided that I wanted to improve the way I did business. I wanted to invest my client's money without the drama of the previous period, give them better service as their financial adviser, so they would have less stress in their life. This had the added benefit that I would have less in mine as well. And to cap it all, I wanted to earn more and work less.

That was my goal. My plan was to focus on what I was good at, which was communication, plus all the knowledge I had built up over many years. I had no idea how I was going to achieve this, but then I didn't need to. I was going to do my bit, have a goal, implement a plan and take action. The Universe would then do the rest.

Within a year I had started to re-position my business; I attracted new contacts, had some fresh ideas and stress levels were decreasing. A few years after that my clients were a lot happier, I was working less, my income had increased and the bonus on top of that was a significant increase in the value of my business.

It is interesting to note that even in later life we still need to relearn our lessons. It is a great reminder that these principles are very real and that can bring huge benefits to us all.

In addition to financial success we need to bear in mind that true success can only be achieved by balancing the other important things in our lives; good health, great relationships and a general feeling of well-being. It is crucial to remember how important it is to truly accept who we are and take really good care of ourselves, which in turn gives us strength and confidence.

Success IS a balance of all these things and this must be our overall aim in life.

Think about our children or our grandchildren; they look forward to each day with anticipation and excitement. They don't have particular expectations; they just get up in the morning and get on with their day. They enjoy all sorts things, big or small. They are quick to laugh (and sometimes cry). They let their emotions out when they need to. Often they are fearless. They don't mind dressing up or dancing in the rain and jumping in puddles.

Similarly, when we are deeply involved in trying to reach a goal, or an activity that is well-suited to our skills, we can experience a happy state of mind. We are going with the flow. We like what we are doing.

I was brought up to believe that we needed to earn the right to be happy; we needed to prove ourselves, but this is back to front.

Happiness is our right and very little can be achieved in life without having this state of well-being first.

Some *Final Thoughts*

It is up to you now. Use all the techniques laid down here and watch your life unfold into something amazing.

We can all do better, whatever the level we are currently at. If we join together, we can all help each other to be better than we were before.

Some Final Thoughts

Perseverance and determination are important factors in achieving anything in life and this is where most people fall down along the journey. However, if our passion is high, and we have a worthwhile goal or goals in life, this will pull us through.

When I realised at the age of 17 that it was up to me, and me alone to make my way in life, everything became clearer. Yes, there have been difficulties along the way, but my determination to succeed was always at the forefront of my mind.

It helps to realise that the 'Law of Attraction' is very real and that there are 'unseen forces' out there that we can use to achieve what we want. As long as we are fair and kind and treat others respectfully these forces will not desert us. We then have a duty to help others less fortunate than ourselves. We can learn to focus on our goals but live in the present; it is all we have, and we can also train ourselves not to dwell on the past as it can derail us.

When we take action, ready or not, the route will be shown to us through our internal Sat Nav.

When we have disappointments, it is all part of our journey to accept and learn from them; everything in life happens for a reason, and after all, if we don't fail along the way we are not trying hard enough. Thomas Edison, who invented the electric light bulb, failed 9,999 times before it was perfected, that's perseverance.

Presented with a problem the response is not: "There is no answer", it is better to think: "There is a way; all I have to do is to find it".

This alone will open our mind and stimulate our subconscious to work it out.

Use affirmations, these are statements to simulate our subconscious mind.

Muhammad Ali, the greatest sportsman of all time said: "I am the greatest". He burnt this statement into his mind consistently over many years, and as a result he became 'The Greatest'.

Have an abundance mindset, by this I mean, expect success, and act as if success were inevitable. Build belief in ourselves.

If we want to be prosperous we need to think prosperity, if we want to be healthy we need to think good health.

Remember again – focus on want you want, not on what you don't want.

It is easy to be put off by others who don't want us to succeed; there are more of them than us so it will take courage to overcome these influences. The TV and press often promote negative reports these days. We need to be informed, of course, but not inundated with these negative influences.

We have a God-given right to be happy, but we may have forgotten this along the way. Let's rekindle the feeling we had as a child.

We have all the tools we need within us, all we need to do is access them as we have discussed.

'Ask and you shall receive' is a phrase from the Bible. Not my words but I do believe them, and why not?

In life we are all responsible for our actions and thoughts and it is up to us to have the life we desire. What makes us who we are is not what we have, it is who we become that's important, and that is up to us and our thinking.

Always promote kindness; if we feel good, we can pass this on to others, and we should never treat others in a manner that would make them feel small.

Our purpose in life is to have bigger goals than those just for ourselves: to be successful so that we can help ourselves first, our families and then those less fortunate.

What is your purpose in life?

My aim in everything I write and in any communication is to help others, particularly children and this is the main purpose of this book.

My wish is that every parent encourages their children to use the philosophies laid down in this book, because with passion and purpose in life we will be happier and more fulfilled.

The final words here mean more to me than anything I have ever read and are the inspiration now for my life going forward......

> *'A hundred years from now it won't matter what my bank account was, the sort of house I lived in, or the kind of car I drove..... but the world may be different because I was important in the life of a child'.*
> Forest E. Witcraft

Let us live a life that is full and fulfilling. Let us be the example and the guiding light for others to follow and in doing this the world will be a better place. Yes, it may take time so let's not hesitate and let us start... NOW!

Thank You and God Bless.

Epilogue

The fact that you have read this book is proof that you have a desire to achieve more in life. However, I suggest you now take action. Action is the only way that these principles can be brought to life and action needs to be continuous and practiced every day, like the athlete in training. Once it becomes second nature it will become a habit and part of your everyday life, and in time become a way of life.

The whole premise of this philosophy and the basis on which it stands is simply the practice of 'FEELING GOOD' every day! If we can do that and pass these GOOD FEELINGS on to others, everything we desire in life can be obtained.

Also by passing this wisdom on to others, the 'story' lives on through the generations.

I have tried to make these concepts as simple as possible, so that even a child can understand and take advantage of them. Hence, I have used the title, 'WISDOM FOR LIFE, IT'S CHILD'S PLAY'.

Throughout my life I have practiced them and refined them and have found it has made a huge difference to what I have achieved in my life and more particularly how I have felt as a person.

We can think of real success, as summed up by Wayne Dyer – ' Being a better person than we were before'.

Let us ALL strive for a better life for ourselves and indeed everyone else, especially our CHILDREN.

Further Information

1. What To Do When All Else Fails and How To Turn Your Life Around
   by Michael Moore
   available at www.blurb.com

2. Mentored by a Millionaire CD set from Nightingale-Conant
   www.nightingale.com

3. The Secret by Rhonda Byrne
   available at www.amazon.co.uk

4. Chicken Soup for the Soul byJack Canfield
   www.jackcanfield.com

5. Think and Grow Rich by Napoleon Hill
   available at www.amazon.co.uk

6. The Science of Getting Rich by Wallace Wattles
   available at www.amazon.co.uk

About the author

Michael Moore is a retired financial adviser who ran his own successful business for more than forty-five years. Over that period he has studied human psychology and personal development and has long pondered on why some people find success in life whilst others struggle.

His passion now, is to help us all, particularly children, to live a more fulfilling and happy life using some simple techniques he has learnt along the way.

With focus and commitment we can all achieve far more of what we want in life rather than what we don't want.

Mike can be contacted at: contact@childsplay.today

www.childsplay.uk.com

My sincere thanks to Lyn Halvorsen, my editor and friend and an author in her own right. Lyn has spent many hours putting this book together. Your help has been invaluable Lyn. Thank you for your support and friendship over many years, it is much appreciated.

Do you want to feel good and feel better every day, achieve more in life and encourage your children to reach for the stars? In this book, Michael Moore passes on his wisdom to us using simple concepts for improving our lives that even a child can understand. It really is '*Child's Play*'.

'Teach your children well'

Every parent should be encouraged to buy a copy for their children

www.polaritypublishing.co.uk

Dedicated to seeking truth and raising consciousness

POLARITY
PUBLISHING

ISBN – 978-1-9995810-1-5

Notes

Notes

Notes

Printed in Poland
by Amazon Fulfillment
Poland Sp. z o.o., Wrocław

51947964R00061